CONQUERED YET VICTORIOUS

SWATI JAISWAL

To,

Aryan

I love you, now and forever.

Contents

Contents

Preface

On the eve of new year, he said "Start writing a little everyday. Maybe something about me too". Guess what? Now, there is a complete book dedicated to you, Aaru.

Acknowledgements

I am deeply gratuitious to Aryan, who made me channel whatever leftover creativity I have, into writing this book.

I would also like to thank my mother for being the most supportive parent one could ever have, and Tannu, for hyping me up to write (and sleep) whenever I felt low or directionless.

Thank you.

Prologue

What it is like to be conquered yet victorious in a realm where our constellations vanquish each other only to rise again...

1. Dandelion and Wildflower

With the heart of a dandelion
you have loved me through thick and thin;
through the worst of storms.
With the passion of a wildflower
you have embraced me in the most broken parts;
in the most crumpled hopes.

2. (was) an ever shifting ocean

i have always been an ever shifting ocean
a pendulum osscilating between two deeply conflicting train
of thoughts
until...
you came in like a tranquil breeze
subtly entreating me to stay-
stay long enough to decide what I really want -
you.

3. silence

my silence dribbles down my lips
mixing with yours like milk and honey
producing unspoken rhythms out of our bodies.

4. art

all my life, i had been throwing away my heart like a two-cent store piece.

when we met, i had no idea you would treat it like an expensive museam art.

5. wild tongue

trace that wild tongue down her body
as she writhes on the bed, the bedsheet crumpling beneath her
it does magic:
making her want you to stop
but making her want to have you more
deeper and harder,
exploring every inch of hers she had kept to be ravaged by
you.

6. (not) happy

i am not really happy
at the parties
or the movies
or the fancy dinners
or the night outs
or the brunches
when i know
i could be with you
just sitting on the bed
doing nothing
but resting my head on your shoulder
while you whispered sweet nothings into my ears

7. what is poetry?

what is poetry?
what really is it?
for me, it is fumbling in the dark,
and floating in the limitless clouds - dark as ashes
trying to find words
that could best describe
what it's like to watch you sleep

8. watch you sleep

maybe if I can't describe how I feel when I watch you sleep, I can describe what I see when you sleep:

You lie on your side of the bed, your head plopped upon the pillow, the covers of which we bought just a few days ago. Your temple lies at ease - free from those lines of stress that form on that beautiful forehead while you're working (sometimes with your tongue out). It's like meeting peace personified, your face as calm as an infant who had been cradled to sleep in the arms of his mother. Your lips pucker slightly when I trace their tips, trying to enclose in my mind what it's like to touch you.

I trace the edge of my finger on your brows and you furrow them, probably because it tickles you. Now, I stretch my palm and cup your face, your

9. chemistry

honestly, i don't know a thing about chemistry
but the way my ribs tingle
the moment your skin brushes mine,
i just know my atoms love yours
and that, my love,
that's chemistry for me.

10. poison

if love was a poison
i'd drink it anyway
if it meant i could love you

11. old love

people believe old love is something that nurtures and grows
with age
people believe old love is determined by how long two people
have been together
people believe old love is tested by time and ups and downs
and everything good and bad before it gets old
i know that's not true
i know i have felt old love when i could do the most
uncomfortable things with you
i know i have felt old love because i never had to find a
"dynamic" with you
i know i have felt old love because we do things, people
otherwise believe, our love isn't old enough to do
i know i have felt old love since the time the time i fell in love
with you.

12. pieces of me

a million pieces of me are with you
those pieces, i believe, must constitute at least half of me
that's why i don't fear losing you
but me, if you are gone.

13. colors on my body

it is often disorienting to think about how your fingers could turn into such amazing paintbrushes, your hands the artists, and my body a diaphanous canvas. you secretly trace your deepest of thoughts on my body from my head to my toe, paint your desire on my lips, and sketch meaningless circles on my back. the further surprising element is that you may as well paint my entire body in your colors and i might still have enough of the white hue to have you fill me in more.

14. lonely shore

i would rather just dive into the ocean
trying to fight for every breath of my life
if i know i could find you somewhere floating in the currents
rather than stay on the safe and lonely shore away from you.

15. when our love has run its couse

when our love has run its course,
(that's how they put it)
stay the night with me
kiss my palm with your fleeting dimpled smile
and dance with me to the song of nothing
until its dawn
and i know i have nothing
but the endless tomorrows -
tomorrows i am meant to spend alone
in a meaningless, restless, and endless agony.

16. desperate

it's dangerous how desperately i could crave just to whiff that scent on your neck and lick it down trying to capture it as a taste on my tongue.

17. home

blue windows
white washed house
a balcony facing the lake
high ceilings
indoor plants
a beautiful garden
it would be everything
but never home without you

18. at the end of the day

at the end,
all i want to be is
an old woman with an old husband
laughing at the absurd jokes
of a wild youth spent together.

19. broken heart

the moment i saw you
i knew you were worth
a broken heart

20. if we met in a club

if we met in a club
dancing to the beats
of the loud music blaring across the room
hands fumbling and groping,
hips grinding,
the moment you would push me
against the wall in a secluded corner
i would suck the moonlight off of your lips
and stumble home drunk off of the taste of you.

21. constellations

i love you like constellations are to be loved-
for their incomplete entirety.

22. sleeping on the couch

but what would i give
to watch you sleeping on the couch
on a lazy Sunday morning
right after we had breakfast.

23. creativity

i feed off of the creativity on his flesh
in fight
in love
and in sex.

24. infinite evenings

some days, i just wish to spend endless and infinite evenings with you:
under a bridge, kissing you with my eyes closed, as the drowning sun mildly caresses every inch of our skin.

25. the truth about magic

the truth about magic is

it does not exist as an independent element

it lives and thrives in people - very rare and very special.

i've seen that magic in you.

26. crazy

it's
crazy
how
i
live
my
life
so
crazily
happy
with
you

27. starving

i was starving to see life
to see light
until i met you.

28. funny thing about poetry

the funny thing about poetry is
it comes out only when i think about you
be it in the darkest of days
or the brightest of starry nights.

29. inevitability

i laugh at the inevitability of it all
how people love you like they should.
how it lights up some of the eyes
and how it dims some down with envy.
i laugh at the inevitability of how you were meant to be *great*

30. better

for a very long time
i thought you deserved better
until one day
i made up my mind to be better for you.
(and trust me, i'll try)